I0392675

THE RIGHT WAY

By John Conley

CREATE SPACE

©2016 by John Conley

Printed in the United States

Contents

ABRAHAM LINCOLN.

Introduction

This is not a book about morality. It is not a book about good behavior versus bad behavior. This is a book about getting your desired result every single time; no matter how many times the task is done. In all things, there exists one procedure of action, which when done correctly and in its proper sequence, yields the result intended every single time. It is the job of a CEO, a football defensive coach, the dishwasher at a restaurant to develop procedures, that when followed step by step produce the desired result.

This book is saying that there is a procedure for winning Oscars; a procedure for the non-violent apprehension of an alleged criminal; a procedure to end wars, just as sure as there is a procedure for tying one's shoes with the result being a perfectly fastened bow every time .

This idea alone is very useful and by itself has the power to change someone's life. But when taken steps further, which will be done in this book, powerful method for action will result.

Currently, we live in a world where there is a low expectation on definite results. By definite, I mean the ideal result being attained again and again without any variation in its outcome. We see this lack of expectation in the products we buy, the services we get and in every facet of life where something or someone does not perform at optimum levels. We see it when we ourselves have great success at a task, only to botch up that same task the next time out.

This book isn't speaking about perfection. For there are no absolutes in this universe, therefore there can be no perfect state. But since we live in a universe of law, i.e. The Law of Gravity, there are consistencies; more importantly there are cycles, repeatable actions that have the same predictable outcome.

Action is the key element to all. Since everything is energy including our thoughts, the actions we take or fail to take determines our results. Action itself brings forth a goal. Action creates. You have to be real with yourself to push beyond any laziness, doubts or anything that will keep you from taking action. Action is vital to getting results. By taking action, you may not get the results you desire, but you will get results. The taking of an action creates an effect.

A method is a plan for attainment. You must be able to create a workable plan and then take action; do the steps of the plan.

If you are not willing to take action, nothing will move. Things that move live. We find death in things that do not move, even the inanimate objects. A thought within itself does contain energy, but if allowed to remain just in one's mind, it dies. You have to put thoughts and ideas out into the physical universe; and the only way you can do this is by taking action. Yes, action has a great chance to attract things one do not want; I.e. ridicule, failure and the likes, but these are just normal to discovering the correct procedure to a thing. True failure is no action taken.

There are many ways to get to a goal. But which gets you to the result that you want every single time? That's the right way. It is the procedure that when done correctly will get you the result every single time.

Life is fair. The strength of the effect you put into your actions will be the measurement of your results. So when you do take action and put in higher amounts of strength, expect great results.

John Conley
29th of July 2016

Chapter One: 1. The Only Reason for Failure

Failure is defined as a lack of success in the direction of an action. This means that one has taken a course of action, but has still not achieved the desired effect that he seeks. Since taking action is a prerequisite to success, one could say that the failure occurred not from taking action, but from the type of actions that were taken. An example of this would be a man setting out to paint his house. He gathers all of the supplies, but instead of using the proper paint brush, he uses his hand to smear the paint on to the wood. In the end, his attempt to paint the house would be seen as a failure, due not to the taking of action; due to the type of action, taken. So as you can see, action is always the right way to go in order to get a product, but then, it is the type of action taken which determines your results.

And it is the same in all things. Take the right action and you get results; take the wrong action and you will fail to get the results. So the reason a man or women fails is because he or she has taken the wrong type of action for the result he or she sought.

So let's see how doing things the wrong way keeps one from getting the results. There's this fisherman who uses gummy worms for bait. Some fish are not willful enough to resist the sugar and artificial favor of a gummy worm, and so the fisherman catches a fish or two. But ask yourself, is this the right way? Just because something works doesn't mean it is the right way.

What is the fisherman's rate of success with this method? How many fishes has he caught this week? The last three months? What is the peak number of fishes captured by way of gummy worm? Upon asking the fisherman, he reveals that he caught way more fish when he used to use live bait like the Earth worm. How many more, you ask? "Oh, round 'bout sixteen, twenty fishes from a single rod. Got so good at it, I had to borrow my sister's husband's three fishing poles. You know he got those real good ones, with little bells on the ends of them that ring each time you get a bite." "So why do you know use gummy worms? You were catching a shit-load of fish per day", you say. "Well the sixteen to twenty fish, I did that in one hour. It was just too fast for me. I use the gummy worms to slow things down. So I don't have to worry about all that jumping' up and down and running from line to line foolishness. I'm retired you know. Fishin's my hobby."

And so there you have it; people do things the wrong way for all sorts of crazy reasons. The first question you have to ask yourself is "what result do I seek? I'm I seeking a half-result, a quarter-result or the full-result?" Those seeking the full-result are the ones that want the job done rightly, look for methods that bring about a complete finish product. So the right way is a step by step method of doing something that when done, it can be deemed a finish product that has been done, by all accounts, correctly.

A steam engine runs off of water and coal. But to keep a modern day car on the road, you have to use gasoline. And the even newer cars and 'fueled' off of only electricity.

In sports, a player must have proper knowledge of the fundamentals in order to score and keep the opponent from scoring. Basketball requires dribbling, passing and shooting the ball with accuracy. Hockey requires the skills of skating on blades, passing and shooting the puck. Soccer is similar to both, but the player must do it with his foot. Each sport has a correct way of doing things to get the proper result. Spike the soccer ball pass the goalie and the ref's blowing his whistle. It is the teams and people who do things the right way in life who succeed. 'Bad teams' are ones that are not operating in the right way and as long as they half-do-it, they will continue to collect failure after failure.

Success in anything is almost guaranteed when it is done in the right way. One's success is also guaranteed when you do things in the right way. Even soothing as trivial as writing an email contains in it a method for the proper way of doing it, in order to get the <u>result</u> one seeks. If you want to write a hateful email and get the recipient to feel the hate, there is a proper way to do that. Many hateful emails contain all capital words like, I HATE YOU. With exclamation points added, I HATE YOU!!!!!!!! The words will be more personal, critical and assigning fault; YOU ARE A TERRIBLE FRIEND!!!!! I BLAME YOU FOR THIS!!!!

The person writing a love letter would make comparisons between the object of his desires and other obvious things of beauty. "Your lips are like baby hands— soft and hard to let go." In the love letter, the writer often will express why he cares about the person and the joy the relationship brings to his life. "I love you because you are fascinating. Your ideas about common, everyday things is expressed and seen from a poet's mind. It is as if I'm in love will the reincarnation of Shakespeare, in a voluminous woman's body."

You want insurance that the next house you paint will cause the neighbor's to stand out in front of it and take pictures? You want Will Smith calling all around town for your phone number because he just read your latest book and wants to star in the movie? Or would you like to have Kim Kardashian sitting at your feet listening to your ideas about fashion? It could happen and it does happen when you do things in the one way that, step by step by mighty step gets you the proper result.

In this book, you will learn how to plot out those steps in your own activities. How to know if they are the correct steps and in the right sequence? You will also learn why we chose to do thing incorrectly. Why a man would rather half-ass it on the job instead of doing the job correctly the first time. You will learn what it takes to keep yourself on the right path that leads to success in any endeavor. How being a rebel often means doing the opposite of what one knows to be correct. And how you can be a rebel who does things in the right way? I will also train you on how to see success patterns in things and how to change unsuccessful patterns. You will learn how to live by truth over falsehood and lies. Why duplication is a heaven sent word, and how that has put Kobe Bryant, Lil Wayne and several others in to the hall of fame of their chosen careers. Then I will conclude with that one way of concluding anything, the right way.

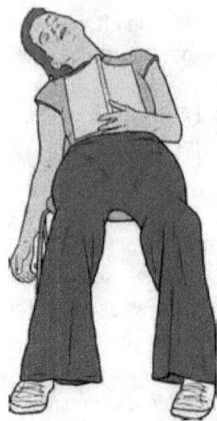

Chapter Two: 2. Laziness (middle-class Mindset)

Laziness Defined

The dictionary defines laziness as follows: 1. Averse or disinclined to work, activity, or exertion; indolent. 1. Causing idleness or indolence: a hot, lazy afternoon. 3. Slow-moving; sluggish: a lazy stream. 4. (Of a livestock brand) placed on its side instead of upright. 5. To laze.

Now, definition number four: '(Of a livestock brand) placed on its side instead of upright.' This one is the closest to my definition of laziness.

Laziness is not doing what one knows should be done.

If you have known the brand should be upright on the cow, then why would you place it on its side?

Imagine the brand on an Apple product being placed upside down instead of right side up? Steve wasn't down with that type of foolishness and you shouldn't be either. People buy books written about Steve Jobs. They watch movies about his life-- And there has been several in the past five year alone. Why? It's because we see Steve Jobs as a man who lived his life doing things the right way. The movies will tell us otherwise; finding flaws in his relationships with others. But, if you were to separate fiction from fact, production from ruin and destruction you will find, Steven Jobs was a man who got things done and he got them done correctly, almost entirely through others. That's a remarkable man. Through all the protesting and temper tantrum most adults do, Steve Jobs pushed through that and made them mutha-'you know what' bring back a product that worked and was done the right way. What's the right way? Anything that can be repeated, over and over at different times and intervals but each time it brings about the same exact result. In other words, you always end up on 34th Street if your original goal was 34th Street. And everyone knows that Miracles happen on 34th Street.

Now how many roads are there to take, in order to get to 34th Street? You can take as many roads are possible, but remember 34th Street is only one street. So the easiest way to get to 34th Street is to get on 34th Street. In other words, what I am saying is that there are several outlying streets that lead to 34th Street, but in this discussion of there being a right way to do anything, keep in mind that there are several to get there, but only one and possible two of those ways will be the correct way.

Like what ways are there to putting a nail into a wall? You could use a shoe, a heavy piece of wood, and I've even seen a man use his bare hand. But the tool for putting a nail into a wall is a hammer; every single time. To use anything else would be the wrong way and a non-optimum result <u>often</u> occurs.

I say often because sometimes you can hit the nail with the shoe and it'll enter the wall perfectly straight. And sometimes, you can hit the nail with a hammer and it ends up bent. But how did this tool we know as the hammer come about? Through trial and error, it was agreed that a metal handle with a flat surface at the end of it was the more accurate way to drive a nail. It is laziness that reduces a tool of value down to an inaccurate pink, six inch pumps.

My own father was a bit of a carpenter. I remember one year he did an extensive facelift on the inside of our apartment. There was one manufacturer's screw that was a complete pain in the butt. Anyone working with a hex screw needs a hex screwdriver! That should a necessity. But my father did not own a hex screwdriver. So what did he use? You guessed it, the tip of a butter knife, the plastic shell of a Bic pen, a regular Slot head screwdriver. In the end, he managed to get the screw tightened, but it took two hours. The butter knife worked best. It kept slipping out of the groove, not to mention the difficulty of getting any torque on it. I spent the bulk of the time chasing down the screw. Each time my father applied pressure on the screw, it would slide out of its seating onto the floor. He finally said the hell with it. The next day, he brought home a newly purchased hex screwdriver.

Per definition number four above, a cattle rancher, instead of branding a cow with the owner's brand visible for all to see, he decides, for whatever reason, (probably because cows kick and scream when you lay them on their back. I'm not talking from experience, just an observation), to brand the cow with the logo askew. Was the rancher rushing?

How many times have you done that? You knew you should've saved that file onto your hard drive before stepping away from the computer to go to the washroom, but you didn't. And when you came back, the battery had died. You lost hours of work. Or what about that time you left a pot on the stove unattended so you could check your Facebook account? When you came back your kitchen resembled that of a forest fire. Again, I'm not talking from experience. No, no, no just an observation.

We all have left windows open, on rainy days; tried to force a 177.2 inch Ford Fairmont into a 10 inch parking space. We've put off going to that restroom before taking that long journey home... Now I've done that. Yes! I'm taking from experience. And more than once might I add. So don't tell me time isn't a factor in the decision to be lazy and put off doing what you should do. All the above are rush jobs. Save some time...

We perceive that time as an extra little, added inconvenience. The time it takes to drive over to the dentist's office to have this cavity check; the time it takes to plan on paper my career as a writer; the time it takes to write down my goals as a young woman graduating from college and entering the work force for the very first time. We all know this one thing about failing to write down your goals-- they don't get done. Life is full of "do me first" activities. Everything in life is more important than everything else. So, when you don't take the time to plan; the time to dream; the time to do something as simple as exercise. They don't get done. Why?

Do you really want me to say it?

La...zi...nessssss.

Laziness is not doing what one knows should be done.

We rather shortcut the time to do it right. But in the end, what we find is that we don't get good products. Plus we end up wasting more time, because we now have to go back and do it right. Or we say "the hell with it" and leave it the way it is. Have you ever seen an unfinished product of any kind? There a person who did it wrong the first time and decided not to go back and do it correctly.

Know this; a non-optimum product is an infliction of harm to you. Anytime you give less than you can give in the doing of a task, you will set a pattern of giving less that will follow you for the rest of your life. Anytime you do the job, but don't do it correctly, you are hurting you. So imagine, twenty, thirty, forty years-- half-assin' it; giving something the barest of the barest minimum. Giving what Homer Simpson affectionally calls, 'The American Way'. Damn!

Most people are unhappy on their jobs. The biggest reason why is because they only do 50% of it when they are on the clock being paid 100% to do it. Go ahead and get mad! REAL TALK. I remember jobs where I did not give my all. But I also remember feeling unfulfilled, unhappy; all of the "un's" were my "un's", and I was unsatisfied with that uncool way of living. Most people hate their manager or supervisor. Why? Because he or she is there to make sure the job gets done, the right way. Their job is on the line when you fail to do your job. So you are not only doing yourself in, you are doing in others around you. "Why should I have to work hard, Sam never does, right"? Isn't that what we hear or some racist, sexist version of it? Someone else not working, equals I shouldn't work, because if I work and he doesn't work, I'm doing his job and my job, both jobs-- no! I just won't work either. Yeah it's a choice. Who does it hurt?

Laziness is not doing what one knows should be done.

I've even seen this taken to the masterful level of complete insanity. I was on this one job where the idea of not working hard because others were not was relevant. It was part of the job culture. Many of the guys who had the deepest attachment to that idea invariably found themselves without a job. But in every case, they had to believe that if Sam was there on the same terms as the rest of us, then that is Sam's business. I'm not going to point it out to the supervisor, I'm not going to say nothing to Sam, and I'm just going to COPY Sam's behavior. Insane, right? INSANE! "So you're going to copy the guy that you were just complaining about not being of help to the group? Now instead of having one guy not pulling his load, we now have two? And, Uh! Now three. Uh! Now six." That's exactly how it went.

Take this with you:

A high level of production tends to boost morale.

So don't worry about Sam.

And as for you supervisor, stay on Sam's ass until Sam either brings up his production or quits. Either way, you will be doing Sam a favor and the group will respect you and raise their production. Not because they fear that what happened to Sam can happen to them. No. They will raise their production because they know it should be done and because it feels so damn good to be a part of the team that's putting it down in the work place. Production boosts moral.

So if you are Sam, what should you do to change that laziness?

You have to observe yourself. Watch your moment by moment reaction to doing what you know should be done. And then do it. Don't wait. Do it! Catch yourself in the laziness and do it anyway. It really is that simple and doesn't require any thought.

We would rather short cut it (time) to save time, but in the end, what we find is that we don't get a good product. And we have to go back and do it the correct way to get the product we were looking through a short cut.

Time is only a factor because we say it is a factor. We go into agreement with everyone else's ideas on how long or how much time it takes to do a certain thing. For example as authors, book writers, screenplay writers, we fall into the trap of believing that it takes a lot of time to craft a screenplay. Just that word, "craft" by itself bring up images of some old furniture builder running his wrinkled but steady hands across the wood finish of a table top. It only took him two years to sand and then re-sand that table again. Now it's ready for the market. Bull! If it took this guy two years to build the freakin' table, then he needs to drill his "craft" and get to moving. "Slow roasted to perfection". Yeah, that may work for coffee, but if the producers of a TV show are handing you the synopsis for the next episode that will air in two weeks, you had better have that episode written in three days. It will take a week to shoot. Another two to three days to rehearse and edit. You have to "get the show on the road" man! You had better be quick about.

The truth of the matter is you are running off of someone else ideas of how long it will take to get a project done. If we would just decide to not agree with the ideas of the slow process, and do it in our own set time, wouldn't we still get it done? Parkinson's Law states, that work expands so as to fill the time available for its completion. Put terms that express time it goes like this, the amount of time that one has to perform a task is the amount of time it will take to complete the task.

So if you give yourself three months to do something as simple as take down the Christmas lights. It will take three months to take down the Christmas lights. You'll procrastinate and put it off for as long as you can. And that's for the guy who has set a time goal (deadline). What of the guy who never even gets that far? Do you thing he ever gets around to removing those Christmas lights? I think not. Set the goal for three months and you will do everything necessary to make that three month prophecy true.

But if you were given an hour to do something that normally would take you three months to do, you would get it done in that hour. You would cut out the entire BS that goes into a three month schedule and you would select out what it takes to get it done in one hour. And you'll get it done in an hour. How many times have you had that high school or college term paper that you were given two weeks to write and you put it off and put it off until the night before it is due? What about that fifteen page biography on Martin Luther King Jr? You buckle down and wrote that thing one hour before class. I've done it. You've done it. You did that. But that's a real life example of deciding for you how long it was going to take to get it done. It was not someone else's idea of how long it should take. It was yours. Why can't we do more of it? Instead of wait to the last minute, get the assignment, rush home and bang that baby out before you kiss the wife good night. Then give it a few days to just sit there. Read over and make as many changes as you like. Then drop it on the desk of your professor or boss, one week before it's due. That's time. You can be a slave to it and follows someone else's idea about how long it takes to do a particular thing, or you can decide for yourself that "it's going to take me, x amount of time to do this" and it will take you that said x amount of time to do it as long as you take action in the direction of that goal.

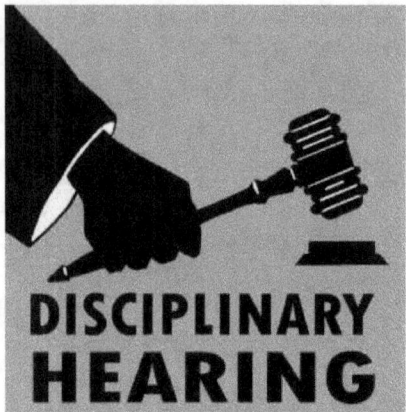

DISCIPLINARY HEARING

Chapter Three: 3. Discipline & Responsibility

There are over ten different definitions in the dictionary for the word discipline. I picked two to share with you.

Discipline:

1. Training to act in accordance with rules; drill.
2. Punishment inflicted by way of correction and training.

Let's look at the first definition and underline a few key words. Discipline: <u>Training</u> to act in accordance with rules; <u>drill</u>.

In order to do things in the right way that will bring results, a person has to condition him or herself to do the actions necessary. One does the actions necessary with discipline.

I will never forget the paradigm shift that occurred in my life during the Summer of 1999. That year, I saw a film that had a great impact on the way I started to see life and the possibilities of life. The film was The Matrix. It was released in theaters on March 31st of that year. I had heard the film's radio ad several times that Spring, but nothing about the ads was appealing. I remember the ads talking about how remarkable the film was, with soundbites from the characters, but like I said I it was not on my must see list.

One day while at a movie theater which was known at the time as the "dollar theater", me and my girlfriend at the time, decided to give this Matrix's movie a try. By that time, people were talking about and since we had seen all the other films the theater had to offer, we figured, why not. MIND BLOWING was this film. Put side the special effects and advancements in cinematography that the film had at the time. When I say mind blowing, I'm literally speaking on my mind being blown away. The ideas presented in this film were a mixture of new age-Buddhist, Laozi, Sun Tzu and Confucianism all rolled into this beautifully crafted story.

What I took away from that movie was this idea that everything that exists in this universal is a pattern. In the film they use the word, "program". The Matrix was about a man, Neo, who could see the world in program language, code, and because he could understand it he could rewrite, bend it to his benefit. After seeing the film, I began to look around and see the various patterns that people, machined, animals operated on. I stated to see the steps and processes of things. Understand that every single thing on this Earth follows some set pattern; until it doesn't. All patterns can be broken; either by design or by circumstances forcing a change.

Here are a few simple examples: A man drinks coffee every single morning as soon as he gets out of bed. He doesn't go to the restroom to brush his teeth and shave, he heads to the kitchen where his auto-coffee maker has a freshly brew pot of hot coffee waiting for him. That's a pattern. One day, he goes to the pot and there is no coffee inside it. He furthers his investigation to find that the power in his part of the city is out. No power, no coffee. Because he refuses to buy coffee from one of those cheap quality, high price coffee chains; he foregoes his day without his pippin' hot cut of joe. The pattern is broken, begrudgingly so.

A woman works at a company where every year no matter how hard she performs she's passed over for a raise during the company's employee evaluation period. That's the Pattern. But this year, she refuses to go quietly into the company's parking garage; she questions her supervisor about it and even hands him her two week notice. She's serious! Shaken by this, the supervisor calls in his manager and they both sit down with her and work out a bonus and increase in wage plan that she is ultimately satisfied with. Patten broken and new pattern set.

The point I'm getting at here is that if you spot a habit in your life that you are unhappy with, you can change it by understanding its pattern and training yourself to do something different. Drill yourself day after day to operate at the new pattern. The more you drill it, the more natural it will become and soon it will become second nature.

Discipline: 2. Punishment inflicted by way of correction and training.

The reason most people hate the thought of inflicting discipline on themselves is because we live in a world where a large number of our institutions are just institutions of discipline. There are strict disciplinarians in our schools. On our jobs: How many of us have grown up with a strict disciplinarian in our homes?

So the word discipline is seen as something to fight back against and protest at all cost. But the best discipline is the discipline that comes from you. Making you do the things that you know you should do is much better than having some eleven foot tall muscle-bound enforcer looking over your shoulder. When you have control of your dos and don'ts, you are in fact much stronger as a person and not much is out of your hands when it comes to controlling your life's direction.

If you fail to discipline yourself in the area of your life where you know you should, life itself will discipline you. We all have heard of the man whose doctor had placed him on a low sodium diet. Or the drunk driver who has been stripped of her driving privileges for failure to abide by the no drinking and driving law. The worst is the criminal who is caught after committing a crime and has to be shipped to a secured location where he is told when to wake, eat and sleep; with no chance of ever returning him until after a judge appointed time has been "served". But discipline doesn't have to get that bad.

You can start off by initiating a small level of control in your life. Instead of driving the car down to the corner store you walk. Then that builds into a bigger action, like taking a walk around the block every day after work. Which then grows to speed walking and before you know it you are flat out running five miles every evening. Discipline does not have to be the enemy.

Duty

RESPONSIBILITY

Responsibility is a funny thing. When you ask the majority of people if they are, most of them will answer back quickly with a definite yes. And in their minds, they really do believe that they are. But when you ask the question, what are you responsible for? Most will say themselves; if they have a family, they will say their wife, the kids; their job. None of it is totally true.

There are levels of responsibility and a great number of people are on the lower end of the scale. No? You can't agree with that? Answer this. If you are responsible for your family, for yourself and your job, then why would you allow wars, nuclear proliferation and a list of worldwide actions that not only jeopardizes mankind, but also the very people and concerns that you yourself say you are responsible for. You are responsible for the entire planet and all that lives on it. There's not a single thing in this universe that each of us is not responsible for.

The right way to approach a project is by taking total responsibility for it. You are responsible if things go right and you are responsible for if things go wrong. It is all in your hands. You are like the heroes from superhero films— all of existence is depending on you. And it's true. All existence is depending on you. Your action, big or small affects others. To get a result in any area, you must be responsible. You must commit to either following the laid out method that works, or developing and laying out your own sequence of actions that work every single time.

You become more responsible by practicing it in everything you do. Have you ever walked down a clean hallway and right there in the middle of the floor was a piece of trash. Now just by quick observation of your surroundings, you can see that the hall is normally spic & span clean, but now there's is one piece of paper staring up at you. Do you pick it up or just walk pass it?

You might debate it, "well, I'm not the janitor." Or you might kick it over to the side out of everybody's way. But did you know that it is your responsibility to keep that hallway clean? Yeah you got a janitor who comes for eight hours every day and stumbles down the place, but you, the resident is responsible for keeping your neighborhood clean and your environment and your planet. Have you ever noticed that if you fail to do it, no one else will? That's why we have some neighborhoods where mile after mile of the community's blocks are populated by discarded trash. Everyone in the neighbor has the attitude that it's not their job, so they don't pick after their neighbors or themselves.

Discipline and Responsibility are the opposite ends of Laziness. They are the tools carried and used, by anyone who is choosing to do things in the right way. There are people who stubble upon success, while being lazy in their actions. There are people who once they get success in a given area grow lazy over time. But to maintain success and to get a true product that works and is effective every single time, you must first take actions. And your actions have to be discipline and responsible ones. I know of no other way to get a workable product.

Chapter Four: 4. the Rebel & Insanity

THE REBEL

I like a good rebel. Most of us do.

The rebel who chases down a would be purse-snatcher, bringing back the victim's purse with an open smile. The rebel who speaks up at the unfair treatment of others, Martin Luther King Jr. comes to mind. The rebel who takes on an entire industry, changing the way things are done; I'm speaking of Sir Richard Branson.

Rebels often have heroism associated to them. They kinda are heroes with the power to resist opposition that wants to stop progress. They have the power to rally others to fight on the side of a good cause. A rebel is a hero because he does and says things that we wish we would have done or said. And he or she does it when the odds are stacked against him or her. Rebels stand up not when they are strong and all power, the do so when enough is enough and when going against the opposition could mean losing everything.

But could being a rebel be a bad thing?

The dictionary define rebel in seven different ways, but the one I'm speaking of is this:

Rebel: rebellious; defiant.

I guess being a rebel could be a bad thing if you are the one being rebelled against. Parents all over word deal with this headache just as soon as their son or daughter hit their teens. So yeah, if you are a parent and your sixteen year old daughter decides to stay out the entire night; you're not going to be too happy about. But the same can be said for the owner of a luxurious apartment building, who despite putting out signs for the tenants and guest not to park their calls in the flowerbed, but they do it anyway. The office kitchen that has signs posted telling the employees to clean up after themselves, but they don't.

A lot of times people rebel not for heroic reason, but just because they don't want to do the work required doing a thing the right way. Normally, this person is Mr. or Mrs. I Know Best. Despite being given proven methods on how to do a thing in a way they consist and gets results, they decide to venture out and do it their way. And more than often they fail. When they do succeed, it is out of luck or forgiving circumstances, when the margin for error was small. A Captain steering his ship on the high seas with nothing on either side of him, will not have a collision problem if he decided to take his eye off the wheel for a few minutes. He very well could throw off his course but the ship wouldn't end up on the rocks. But let that same Captain release the wheel for a few seconds while pulling into the docks. Now you have a major catastrophe, with coast guards and all.

So some rebellious stands are not only damaging but they are largely irresponsible. When the right way has been discovered either through extensive research or trial and error, one should not try and defy them and strikeout on one's own. He should follow it to the letter and change nothing. For the moment a change is introduced into a carefully laid out sequence, failure is the result.

This is how simple this could be. You have a lady who must be at worker every day at 7am. It is important that she is there at 7am because she opens the store for all the other employees; she is the only one with the keys. This lady has a successful pattern of being out the door by 6:05am and at the bus stop by 6:15am. The bus stop is less than a five minute walk from her apartment and she normally makes it there with lots of time to spare. But on this particular day, she introduces a change in her "successful" pattern. Instead of going directly to the bus stop, she stops at a coffee shop. She gets to the bus stop only to find that the bus has taken off without her. She's late for opening up the store.

Another example would be a farmer, who for several years has planted two acres of corn. This has always brought him success even during time when weather conditions were not favorable. But one year, he decides he's not going to do it that way. All he ever really needed was one acre of corn to feed his family for the year and sell down at the local farmers market for a year salary of $50,000. He figures if he plants less he's be saving money on the cost of seeds, water not to mention that it would be less work. He would only have to plow and tend one acre of land instead of two. So he changes his success pattern. And by the end of the year, he has to file for government assistance to feed his family. Part of the one acre of corn he planted was eaten by crows, some of the seeds failed to sprout and what was left went towards feeding the family. There was none left to sell. The farm violated a successful action, and he and his family paid the price.

Both of the above examples are not over the top rebel off his rocker kinds of scenarios, but they are not to prove a point. Large or small, the changes in a pattern that is success equals an occurring failure. It doesn't matter if the failure is "oh she just missed the 6:15 bus, there's a 6:30 but. She'll only be one minute late from opening the shop. The change in a pattern that works means that it will not work. Sometimes not being rebellious simply means following a set recipe. Not deviating from it.

Isn't that Right? Cooking is like that. Failure to follow the proper measurements and the food tastes different. It has to. Life has scales, exactness, degrees and estimations. Get them wrong, BOOM!

This so obvious in the sciences where a mixture of this with too much of a mixture of that can be fatal. This is also the case when following a successful action.

Are there some successfully proven actions that fail? Of course. Something that worked yesterday may not work in the same way today. Yesterday, the bus was at the stop at 6:15am, but today the bus got there at 6:10am, traffic was light. But 6:15am is the norm.

Some successful actions change due to changing circumstances. Light traffic, means the bus will arrive soon. Heavy traffic, expect the bus to arrive late. Factors do exist that changes things. We live in a world of change. The world is flat today, tomorrow its round. Change; changes are inevitable. So no, not every pattern is going to work forever without error. But theoretically, if one was to follow the pattern exactly and no change of any kind was introduced in the situation, then every-single-time the result would be the same. So you must spot the changes that have or will occur and make adjustment. But when given a sequence of steps that brings results and all the conditions around are stable to suddenly introduce change into the equation is suicidal and insane.

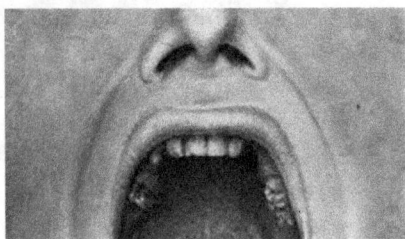

INSANITY

Definition: Insanity - a condition of being insane; a derangement of the mind.

If it is not broke, don't try and fix it.

How strange would it be to see a fire engine rushing to a home, hosing it down and pulling the occupants from the home where there is no fire. Insane right?

This kind of insanity happens every day in offices, homes government institutions across this planet. Laws that work and protect its citizens are changed; so are procedures in the office place. A harmonious home is thrown in disarray when a husband introduces a change that takes his wife off guard. In the eighth round, a boxer switches up the fighting strategy which won him the other previous rounds and is knocked out cold. Life knocks out those insane enough to change something that was working.

We see this lot of times in a marriage. A young married couple is doing financially well. They are emotionally happy. Together, they seem to have the world at their feet. Then one day, either gets curious or wonders what it would be like to be with someone else outside the marriage. She or he switches sides, hoping to find the same happiness if not better with the new spouse he or she left the previous one for and the relationship not only goes shipwreck, but so does his or her life and many times so does the life of the previous spouse.

It happens also in the area of successful business partnerships. Groups with a solid understanding of business success come together and take the business world by storm, together. And then they break apart and they are successful, but not on the level they were when a team.

Singing groups are the worst. You get a Michael Jackson and the Jackson Five... well wait. Michael was even far more successful on his own. So was Justin Timberlake, bad example. But sometimes, a group is super successful mainly because of one of its members. I think it is safe to say that Michael Jackson was the most popular member of the Jackson Five and was Justin Timberlake, they were the lead signers and for good reasons, they both are/were super talented men. In other words, the formula for the success of the Jackson Five or NSYNC was largely built around their lead singer.

TWO KINDS OF REBELS

There are two types that break the rules.

1. The guy or gal who wants to fail either aware or unaware of this desire.

2. The guy who is in search or attempting to do things in the right way, but has not yet found or developed a working method.

The Guy or Gal Who Wants To Fail

Believe it or not, there are people who set themselves up for failure. Sometimes they are hard to detect. They may dress very well often, and have been to the best colleges and universities, so they say. But look closer... what is this person's success rate? How often has this person failed (big or small) since you know him or her?

You have a guy who is seemingly working hard to achieve some goal, but continuously comes to a roadblock. This person seems to never be able to catch a break. They are always complaining about not being able to catch a break and he or she has a negative thought and speech patter about the world and its cruelty.

This person often is not only set on taking his or herself down, he or she also pulls those around down with him. He or she also drains the energy of those around, causing them, if they are not careful to become pessimistic and as insidious as her. I speak from experience and believe me, when I say that this type of person will suck you dry and leave you on the roadside for dead. They are not to be taken lightly.

The Guy or Gal Who Wants To Succeed

This person will make mistakes. Fail. But he or she is failing by trial and error. He is looking for the correct formula for which to go by. Once he finds that formula, seldom does he change it. Changes only occur when he allows The Guy or Gal Who Wants to fail to enter his life to "help". Association with these people creates the doubt that leads him to change successful actions.

The Guy or Gal Who Wants to Succeed would do well to remember the old farmer's adage, "if it isn't broke, don't try to fix it." This, along with the knowledge, that there are those floating on the sea of life that is looking to take as many people down with them as possible.

Chapter Five: 5. Seeing Patterns

Earlier I spoke of the film, The Matrix, and how that film got me to see the patterns in things. Well if you don't already see in patterns this chapter will hopefully change that.

There are many definitions of Pattern, but the two that will help you here are as follows:

1. A combination of qualities, acts, tendencies, etc., forming a consistent or characteristic arrangement.

2. An original or model considered for of deserving of imitation.

Here is a list of Patterns per definition number 1:

Definition # 1: Pattern - A combination of qualities, acts, tendencies, etc., forming a consistent or characteristic arrangement.

A: Patterns

* Life on the Mississippi River: The rapid, flowing currents; ducks, gators, bald eagles and snakes.

* Elementary School: Books, chalkboards, desk, students and teachers.

* Five Star Restaurant: Busboys, uniformed waiters, artistic plates of food, and customers and in expensive evening wear, men suits, ladies skirts and dresses.

This patterns about fit their settings. We would expect to see those things when visiting the actual locations. Now take a look at the pattern below.

B: Patterns

* Life on the Mississippi River: Flowing currents, ducks, fifth foot tall space ships, gators, bald eagles, Martians and snakes.

* Elementary School: Books, chalkboards, desks, students and a interactive computer screen.

* Five Star Restaurant: Busboys, uniformed waiters, artistic plates of live human body parts. Yikes!

See the difference? There is an element in each of the above that does not fit the pattern. The first of the above is something out of a Science Fiction book, and the second one is a bit of a prediction for the future and the last is a scene out of a Zombie film; If Zombies Ruled The World. The above patterns could be said to be odd or unworkable with the fluky items in place. This goes to prove that there are recognizable pattern that exist and we see those patterns as successful representations of themselves. Throw a curve at such patterns and they are sometimes hard to digest and are doomed for failure.

Here are some patterns for definition number 2:

Definition # 2: Pattern - An original or model considered for of deserving of imitation.

A Pattern:

* Assembly Line. Currently used by several organizations. The first use of it in America is credited to Henry Ford, of the Ford Motor Company.

* Story: Beginning, Middle and an End.

* Fashion. Speaking of Michael Jackson, remember the red leather jacket with the entire zipper? His effect on pop culture was felt around the world and many saw him as deserving of imitation.

Go from a gradient of ease to spot patterns to more difficult and complicated patterns.

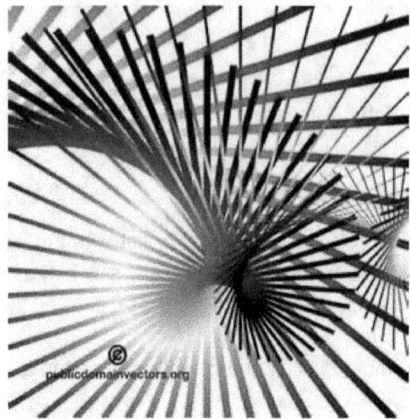

Chapter Six: 6. Changing Patterns

Changing a set pattern is not always the best thing to do, and I for the most part do not condone it. But I do suggest adapting patterns. In other words, taking a pattern from one area and using it elsewhere. One can use a pattern as a template to work out a situation in another area to get successful results. If a pattern is successful in one area, there is the chance that it can be successful in others. It is taking something that works in one area and applying it to another area to achieve similar success.

I'm not talking about changing the structure or sequence of things. What I'm talking about is using successful models from other sources. Example: An owner of a car dealership walks inside an Apple Store. The store is crowded with customers who are there to use the products without pressure to buy. He gets the idea to take that model to his dealership. He paves a grassy part of the property and puts in a mid-speed race track. He fills his showroom with young twenty-something employees in jeans and t-shirts and opens the showroom cars up for customers to hop inside and get a feel for spending some time behind the wheel. Customers take solo test drives around the track in replica cars similar to the one that are for sale on the lot.

Like Apple, a constant inflow of customers populates the dealership. Classes are given

It is also taking some area where you have a great deal of familiarity and applying it to an area where you have only a basic level of knowledge. You are looking for relatable area so as to fully understand the area you do not know. This is a comparative method.

This method could also be used to spice things up in a particular area and to make things more interesting. The above car dealership would be more interesting than your normal dealership.

How Do You Change a Pattern?

The first thing you must do is identify what you have and its purpose. Let's say you have a table; just your common four leg table. The purpose of a table is to hold something on top.

Next, you define all of the elements that make up the table and the reason for each. The top of the table is flat, that is the table's surface. It stays flat and its use is to hold other flat objects. With a table, you also have something to hold the surface in place called legs. The standard table has four legs.

So the pattern of a table is a flat surface with four legs holding it steady. From your examination of the table, you quickly come to see that the base of the table is the most important part of the table in terms of keeping it safe and stable. From your knowledge of how the table works, you design your own style of a table.

The purpose of a chair is to hold a person's body steady while in a seated position. There are so many various use of the chair: lounge chairs, stools, a bench.

Chapter Seven: 7. Truth over Falsehood

Truth is facts. It is information that can be proven and used to make decisions, calculate one's next move or draw one's conclusion. With truth, the result one says is to what he had gotten. Truth is the reality of something; it is the actual state of something. Truth is also everyone's agreement about a thing or subject. There was a time when the majority of people in a certain part of the country called Salem, who believed that women were witches working for Satan. A lot of women were murdered because of this false belief. Truth is in fact, actual.

When wrong information is fed to a person, information that is based on opinion, prejudice or someone's distorted misunderstanding of things, mistakes and failures are made. One of the biggest causes of a person's failure can be found in having false information. Falsehood is not in fact, actual.

Pattern that works is truth. It is an actual thing that each time you use it you get the same result.

Chapter Eight: 8. One Line of Action

Okay one line of action. What do I mean by one line of action?

At one point in time, you have the Current Scene, the way things are right now at this moment. At the far end of the spectrum, you have the End Scene, end goal. So the first step you take is you write down the End Scene. What is it? What does it look like? How are you going to feel when you get it? Right everything you can down about the End Scene.

Next is the Current Scene, how things are right now. You write it down. Present a clear picture of what your current life is, looks like— all the little details. You also write down the emotion of it. What do you feel in this current state?

Once you get both down as clearly and as succinct as possible, the next step is to place in all the steps that take you from the Current Scene to the End Scene. Write down each step you need to take. These steps are not detailed steps; they are the big picture steps needed to get an area of work done so that you move into the next area of work, working your way to be End scene.

Here is an example of what I mean: let's say you have a bike that you would like to ride to the park. So your End Scene would be you in the park with the bike. Your Current Scene would be the bike in its current condition. Now let's say that the current condition is that the bike is on a flat.

What are the steps that you need to take to get you from the current scene, of the bike being on a flat, to the end scene, of you in the park with the bike. The first step you would take would be to identify what needs to be done to fix the flat. So step one would be you identifying the problem. Let's say the flat has a big gaping hole in it. So you decide that you're going to need a new inner-tube. Step two, go to the store and purchase a new inner-tube.

Now all the little details of you going to the store you do not write in the step, because they are just details that are not needed. After you come from the store with the inner to purchase, step three would be inserting the new inner tube. Step four would be to put into the tire. Step five would be to ride the bike to the park and your final step would be you, in your End Scene at the park.

The trick to doing this is to work your way back from the End Scene. This is a process known by many as reverse engineering. Where you start with the end in mind and work your way back. This is a sequence process so you want to make sure that each step leads to the next step in order. If it's not done in order A equals B equals C equals D as the next step, then the process is been done wrongly, and you must go back and rearrange the steps so that they fall under a synchronized pattern. Sometimes, you will not know that a step is out of sequence when you first write it down. But as you go through the steps in real life, you will see when something's not in his proper place. At that point, you can rearrange the steps to fit in sequence.

This is another example. The guy wants to open a pizza shop. Doesn't know anyone he doesn't have the connections. But what he does know how to do his chart things out in of line of action. So the first step he would take would be to write down the End Scene. He would get a clear picture of what that End Scene should be like. What it feels like in all the details associated with. Then he would write down the current scene, what things are right now with all the details. Next, he would step by step layout the sequence of events he needs to take to get from the beginning of the spectrum to the very end.

Let's say that this man's End Scene is him in the pizza shop surrounded by customers and he's whirling pizza dough into the air. Let's say that his beginning scene is him standing in his kitchen with the idea. So his first step if we worked from backwards would be him standing in front of the store cutting the ribbon for the grand opening. The next step in reverse order would be him promoting the business to others, letting them know about the grand opening. The next in reverse order would be him hiring and training the staff.

Next would be buying the supplies. Next in reverse order, would be building any additional workspaces and cleaning the store, getting it ready for business. The next step, rent out or buy a location. Step that will precede that would be to get the funds and licenses needed to run a pizza place. Before that, he would have to find out how much it cost and what license are needed to run a pizza parlor. And that leads us back to the Current Scene.

AVOIDING ABERRATION

Aberration is departure from a straight line of action. I would like for you to look at a straight line of action as going from a point to a B point, because in the end that's what you are attempting to do. You are attempting to go from where you are right now to the goal that you have in mind. In order to do that, you don't have to be focused in only on what you are trying to achieve, but you must also stay committed to that line of action once plotted out and let nothing unrelated to his achievement push you or sway you towards a different path.

This is what happens to most people when they set an End Scene: they began moving in that direction and then someone or something comes along and says you should be over there. "Over there" is a point that takes them off of the straight line from point A to point B. More specifically, aberration is moving in zig-zag line, never reaching the end goal or if it is reached, a great deal of time has been wasted.

It looks like this:

Imagine a football player on the 5 yard line, ready to run the ball into the in zone. He's handed the ball and instead of running right up the middle through as many defenders as possible, he runs instead to the left, back to the right, then back to left, to the right, to the left, to the right, and finally he's tackled on the 1 yard line.

Now if he had used his energy and the protection of his defense to run straight ahead from where he was in a point, to the end zone, a B point he would've made the touchdown in less time exerting less energy. How many times in life do we see family and friends running all around when all they need to do is plot there End Scene and their starting point, place in the sequenced steps needed to get from one point to the next and diligently move ahead. Not allowing anything to distract them or to take them off their line of action.

FOCUS

Whenever something comes up that will command an amount of your time, just ask yourself, "will this lead to me achieving my End Scene?" If the answer is no, then you don't do it. For many that sound harsh and I must admit that for many years, I thought the same. But what is harsher is you staring in the mirror at yourself five years from now, 10 years from now and not having achieved the important goal that you wanted to achieve.

When I say important goal, what I mean is that you can set of line of action for anything, but is the life goals, the things that you wouldn't be happy in life unless you achieve them; those are the subject of this chapter. We all have dreams. We all have things that we want to achieve in our lifetimes. Life itself is a distraction from us achieving those dreams. The people and the different circumstances in life will pull you further and further away from your dreams unless you set a line of action and follow it. Learn to say no. Learn to not allow anything to take you off your course of action. And I promise you that you will achieve it. You will learn the things you need to learn. You will meet the people you need to meet. You will find the money and all the circumstances needed to achieve your life train if you stay on the line of action. When you don't stay on the line, it is no one's fault but your own. And that's a hard pill for some people to swallow.

They blame others when they don't achieve their dreams. But when you really dig deep, when you really look at the reasons why you are not achieving the goals and dreams you set out to achieve. It's you. Other people will be obstacles. Other people will do things to pull you off the line; most certainly.

But who allowed them to do it? If you cannot see that it's you, then there's no way you can correct. Saying that is someone else makes you victim to their whims. It makes you out-of-control. And if you're out of control, then how could you steer yourself to your goals? You can't. But when you know that it's your hand that is on that steering wheel. And it's your hand that made the right turn or the left turn that took you off course. And it's your hand that can steer you back in the right direction.

When you are on the path, there will be obstacles. Your job is to make sure that the sequence of steps you created that will lead you towards the end goal are the correct steps and are in the right sequence. If they are continue to move ahead despite any obstacle that may be there. What happens if your steps in sequence are correct is that the obstacle will move out of your way. Sometimes, you just have to endure. Let me say that again, sometimes YOU JUST HAVE TO ENDURE. We see this a lot, a person runs up against an obstacle there on the right path, but as an obstacle standing in front of. Most people instead of fighting their way out of the obstacles change path or give up altogether. Then they go around telling people that what they did just didn't work, but what actually happened is that they were moving in the right direction and then an obstacle came along and that's what stopped him. The best way to look at this is to look at it from a story point of view. In stories, you have a character, the character has a goal that they're trying to reach and you have obstacles to the character reaching that goal. It's the mark of a bad story when a character starts with one goal and switches his goal due to the problems he faces alone the way. Think about that. Think of your favorite movie and look at the hero. Did the hero have a goal at the start that was changed because of some obstacle or did the hero maintain the goal he was pushing towards and overcoming obstacles? See stories are about heroes who overcome obstacles. Real life is mostly about people who give up because of obstacles. This is the reason why stories about heroes are popular in our society. The majority want to be like the hero. Heroes don't watch stories about heroes. Why would they. It would be like watching a story about yourself, where you know what's going to happen next because you have done through it. Heroes are that way.

You avoid aberration by sticking to the script. You do not deviate from the plan that you have charted out. Along the way, there will be obstacles, better and faster ways to do things, and steps not previously considered. You can make changes as long as those changes lead and fit on your line of action. In other words, if a new action or new change takes you off your line of action, it is an aberration; you should avoid it. Just imagine driving a car. The moment you take your attention off the road is the moment you end up off the road. So in order to stay on the road in life where you're trying to go or want to be, you must focus and keep your hand on the steering wheel and give it some gas. It really is that simple.

My example is that for many years, I have sought out to be a paid writer in the film and television industry. Originally I had no line of action. I knew where I wanted to go I somehow had an idea of how to get there. But I did not plot out the sequences. And so, I did not have a well-defined line to follow. So every single offer that I got to do other things that would take me in several different directions, I did. All of the directions were good intentioned directions. Directions that was helpful to others. But in terms of me achieving the goal that I set out to achieve, the deviations were all aberrations to my own plan and desire. I do not advocate not helping others. I think one of the greatest things you can do is to help others. But if helping others hurt, put off, seriously delay your plans then you have to decide for yourself whether to help over your own goals and plans or to continue on your line of action and come back and help once your goal has been achieved. Because I personally found out that it is more difficult for me to help someone else when I neglected helping myself.

Learning to say No is one of the greatest skills you can learn.

You do not want to have more than seven steps that way you keep it simple. Seven steps that get you from the beginning point to the End Point. You don't want to have anything less than three.

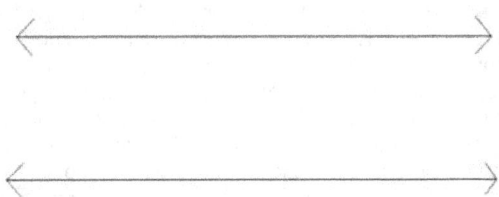

GOALS THAT RUN PARALLEL TO YOUR OWN

A lot of times we see this, a man or woman who has a goal, ultimate goal who seems to be off the path to that goal, but in the end, they end up with the goal achieved. Here is an example: a guy wants to be a world-champion cyclist and that's his End Scene (2 world champion cyclist titles). But he works at a bike shop. So every day for eight hours, he's selling or fixing bikes. This can be a goal that runs parallel to his dream. The goal for this line of action is to make enough money to buy an excellent bike that he can race with at the Tour de France. So he works at the shop for a number of years, saving his money, learning about bikes, (the best ones to buy), and meeting other cyclists who are good at the sport. Meanwhile on the line of action of his dream his first step is to cycle in a local marathon. His next step is to compete in a cycling contest and win. He's met with obstacles; he loses the first two contests he enters. From this, he learns a thing or two and wins the next three contests. His next step is to get sponsorship. Because he works at the bike shop, the bike shop sponsors. His next step is to get a major sponsor. Again because he works at the bike shop, he meets a major vendor. The vendor sponsors his trip to the Tour de France. His next step is to enter the Tour de France which he does. He competes and loses. But again, he gains knowledge that will help him in the future. His sponsorship continues to support and after a year of training, he competes again and when the Tour de France commences, he enters again and after four years of defeat he wins his second Tour de France; his goal is complete. In a parallel goal, there is the appearance that one is not working directly towards his dream but as long as the parallel goal intercepts at some point with the major dream goal, then one is on the correct path. The parallel route is only to be used in situations where one has to take the back door because he knows no one or some other extreme circumstances.

Be careful not to trick yourself into believing that those of others are parallel to your goals. Here's something I used to do as a writer. I would set goals for completed stories, stories that I would write myself. And someone would come along and pitch me their story and I would think that this is a good project to work on, and I would make up all the excuses of why I should work on it I.e. two heads are better than one, double our speed, double our contacts. Plus I would see that working on their projects was still parallel to my overall dream of a writer. But what eventually would happen is that I will put off my project to finish the collaboration project, and either person I collaborated with would give up and stop pushing the project or not push the project from start. So I would spend a lot of time and energy pushing a project that I co-wrote or developed with someone else. Eventually I stopped pushing the project either out of frustration or because I felt it was unfair. But when I walked away from it, it was no longer a project that I can count as my own. So in other words, I could not show it around town. So as far as the industry was concerned, I hadn't written anything because I hadn't written anything that was my own. And to me, several years to learn this and a lot of wasted time. So be careful when you find projects where you have to work with others to achieve a goal. Ask yourself, "If I do this project, what percentage of ownership do I walk away with? If it's not the majority ownership, you should do it. The reason I say this is because if you have majority ownership and you can dictate where the project goes and not have to wait for someone else to give you everything, it's okay. But in the writing game, my advice would be to not co-write anything.

Chapter Nine: 9. Duplication

DUPLICATION & IMITATION

To duplicate, is to copy the way something is done. To do it like you have seen it done. When you think about it, the majority of our training in life from the alphabets to on-the-job training is all taught through imitation— duplication. Our first attempt at duplicating is not always spot on. We make mistakes as we learn. But like duplication, the more we duplicate the duplications in our imitations, the better we get at whatever we are attempting to duplicate.

Have you ever tried to duplicate a song that you heard for the very first time? You will get the words wrong blurt out the incorrect melodies, but the more times you listen attentively to the song, the easier it becomes to duplicate it. The same is true with anything. The more often you do a thing, the better you get at imitating that thing. A baseball player learning to consistently hit the ball is just duplicating the swing. The more often he duplicates that swing, the more natural the swing becomes and the more likely his chances are that he would hit the ball in the unforeseen future. Throughout a NBA season, players get to know other players style of play plus they watch video of players and the teams they play against. Watching the video is a form of duplication that teaches the player how to defend against the opposing team. Practice is all about duplicating plays and other successful actions. The play book is practiced over and over until the players can do it without thinking about it.

Even in our education system, we are taught through duplication and imitation; the alphabets, learning to count to one hundred, languages all through duplication and imitation. The difference between duplication and imitation is that imitation is going through the motions of doing it the way you saw it done. Duplication is to be spot on in the way you saw it done. So in duplicating something, you are being exact and you are doing it just like it was originally done. Now imitation can often get a bad name. Because imitation is doing something more like the original, but the performance is not on point. So when others see it, they feel like you're imitating something else. A duplication of that thing would be so well done that they would almost believe it is the original.

Roger Bannister, Olympic middle distance runner in 1954 ran the mile in four minutes. It was the first time in Olympic history that it had ever been done. Not soon after others begin running the mile in four minutes. This is an example of how imitation is done, leading to duplication and next to elevation.

IMITATION — DUPLICATION — ELEVATION

When one sets out to imitate something once, he imitates it if he likes he can stop right there. An example of this would be a person who hears a song and learns the lyrics to the song. Now he can sing it whenever he chooses to knowing that he will be lyrically correct. But if he wants to go a step further, he begins to imitate the pitches of the original singer. He imitates the inflection in the voice of the singer. Even go so far as to imitate the mannerisms of the singular as he sings the song. All of these imitations combine and done over and over again with practice will lead the imitator to duplicate this singer. But once the duplication is done, he doesn't have to stop there either. He can elevate it. Elevation is done by adding one's own key signature to something in a way that advances it. The word elevation means to raise or lift something to a higher position. For this example, I'm going to go to the art known as rap or hip-hop music.

In the 1960s, boxer Mohammed Ali influenced the next-generation when he began reciting lyrical predictions about the outcome of his fights. His comical trash talk would soon be imitated by young New York ghetto kids who wanted to imitate their idol. Soon in the 1970s, block parties became the thing in New York City and throughout inner-city ghettos. Often at these parties a MC, master of ceremonies, would host a party and serve as the hype man for the DJ. The first recorded rap song was the Sugar Hill Gang's "Rapper's Delight". That one song led to others imitating the style and rhythm of the music. As time progressed, the simple rap style that was practiced in the 1970s became more complicated, more lyrical, with the beats more dynamic. If you were to listen to "Rapper's Delight" and compare it to "Otis" by Jay-Z and Kanye West, you would see just how much rap music has been elevated. What has elevated the genre of rap music is faster beats faster wrap styles or flows in more complicated string together of lyrics.

The desktop computer, the cell phone even the automobile with cars like the Tesla are all elevations of the duplicated original that imitated something else. The first car was an imitation of the horse and buggy. The first phone was an imitation of the canned phone where you hook up two cans to a piece of screen and run it over long distance and transfer sound from one can to the next. The computer was in imitation of the basic calculator. Each advanced. Each was an elevation.

WHAT SHOULD YOU DUPLICATE

You should duplicate successful actions. Anytime you find in your field someone who does a thing to a higher height, it behooves you to study that person and figure out the key elements he or she uses to the successful. What is his or hers line of action when it comes to doing that thing; if you learn that and study it, you too can become just as great. But in studying it, you must make sure that you duplicate what they do, the sequence of steps, and be careful not to imitate what they do. The imitation of greatness is not greatness itself, it is a watered down version of greatness. But a duplication of greatness is the greatness.

KOBE BRYANT

Upon entering the NBA in 1996 Kobe Bryant like so many others idolized Michael Jordan. But unlike so many others who often would <u>imitate</u> Michael Jordan's style of play. Kobe Bryant managed to duplicate. If you don't believe me, all you have to do is go to YouTube and watch the comparison video of Michael Jordan and Kobe Bryant. In that video, you will see back-to-back moves first done by Jordan then duplicated by Kobe Bryant. Kobe is the perfect example of how a person should duplicate greatness in order to be great themselves. I have heard it said that Kobe Bryant was less of a player because he duplicated Michael Jordan. I disagree. It takes a great amount of intelligence, a high IQ, and hours and hours of practice and study to duplicate anything. Kobe Bryant, unlike in the other player who try to imitate Michael Jordan, got it right to the point that Kobe has stats that are greater than Michael Jordan's career stats.

HOW TO DUPLICATE

To begin with, you find something that you think is worth <u>imitating</u>. Secondly, you write down the End Scene of the imitation and the Starting Point. Thirdly, you write down all of the in-between steps of the imitation. Once you have everything in their correct sequence, you practice. You drill it over and over until you are no longer imitating it; you have complete duplication of it. The speed in which you move from imitation to duplication depends on the person. Some people will pick it up faster than others. This simple technique will also help to boost your IQ, because after a while you will start to see the patterns in other things. Once you are able to see patterns, which means you are just able to look at something and duplicate how it is done, your IQ increases because IQ is all about a person's speed in recognizing the patterns in things. The IQ test is the measure of a person's reasoning ability. It is the ability to solve problems quickly. IQ stands for Intelligence Quotient. The quicker one can see the patterns in things, the quicker you understand how the thing works and the quicker you are able to solve any problem associated with it. This takes awareness. Awareness is increased by doing the duplication steps mentioned above. The more your do it, the more aware you become of how something is put together and soon you will start seeing the same patterns in other things. People who are referred to a genius are people who recognize patterns quicker than others. For the ones who are not geniuses, the patterns have to often pointed out before they can see it, and often they still do not see or recognize the patterns.

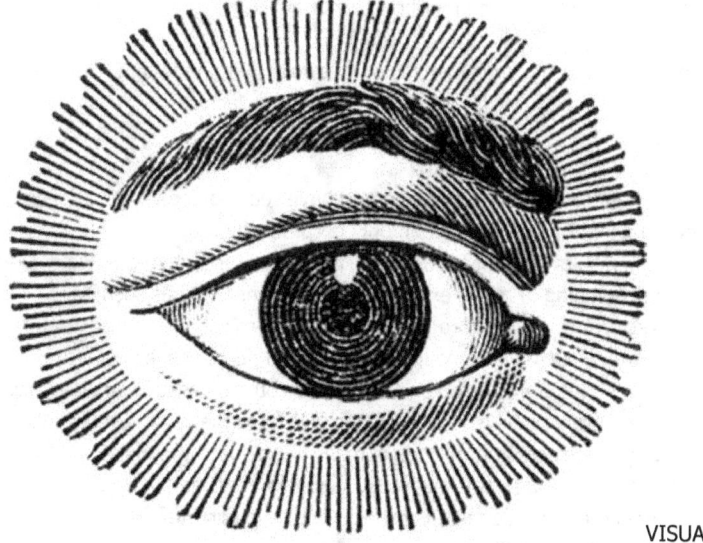

VISUALIZING

Right here I just want to say a few things about visualizing. Visualizing is another way to make your imitation turn into duplication much faster. Whenever you cannot do the physical action of the imitation you should do the visualizing of it in your mind. Now how is that done? Let's say you are a successful businessman, but one of your weaknesses is doing meetings where you pitch ideas. Now you have already done the work of studying someone who successfully pitches ideas. You have broken down the technique and you have the steps laid out. You practice that is much as you can when you encounter your own meetings. But doing the times when you're not in meeting pitching ideas, you do it in your mind. So the successful businessman would see himself going through the process step-by-step successfully pitching in his mind. And he would do it to a point where it feels real, being real to him is not just an exercise he sends to the faces of the people and get their responses. He can feel the floor beneath his feet. If he does that, it is just like the real thing. It's a simulation of the real thing. So that's what you do when you cannot do it in reality.

WHAT TO DUPLICATE

Principles - a fundamental truth; a rule or natural law; something that is a basic truth that is a foundation for a system of behavior or belief.

Skills - a practical ability to do something successfully that one is competent in.

WHY DUPLICATE

Because you want to achieve results that you have seen someone else achieve. This is the reason we imitate. The imitation only becomes duplication when we decide that we want those results to consistently mimic the person or system that we chose to imitate. From the beginning of man's existence on this planet, he has seemed to succeed. He has sought to survive through success. Success is the true measure of survival and how well a person is doing in life. Successful people have successful actions. Their actions are often studied and imitated by others because others realize that if they followed a successful person they may also have the same level of success. This is a smart way of looking at it, but not so many people take the imitation to the level of duplication. Once you start to duplicate, you have reached a level of mastery in that area, so your success will be more consistent and much greater than the person who is just imitating. We duplicate because we want consistent results from our actions. We duplicate because we not only want to imitate the actions, but we also want to embody it and make it a part of ourselves. We duplicate because we have studied and practiced to the point where it now is a natural part of us.

PRACTICE

Practice is a drill. It is doing the same thing over and over, correctly, until it becomes natural. The best way to practice is to break down the practice in each little part or step from your action line. Once you get the steps down where you know how to do them and you have practiced them several times, then you can practice doing the overall line of action without stopping. That way, you lock it in first having complete mastery of the individual steps and then you combine the steps to complete the entire line of action and then you practice the entire line of action over and over until you can duplicate without flaw.

Practice plays a big part in being able to duplicate anything. If one fails to practice the thing that he's imitating, he will never reach the level of complete duplication. I've noticed that NBA player, baseball players, and football players, as well as soccer and every other sport these players and their teams practice more than they play in the actual game; is the secret to be uncovered here. If one was to practice in his chosen field more than he actually played or did it for real, he would become a pro at it. For example, in basketball, the players practice drills. They'll shoot the ball from the foul line thirty to one hundred times during a practice drill. This is done to prepare them to make free throws in the actual game where they may only shoot a free throw five or six times throughout the game. But it is the practice of doing it repeatedly as a practice drill that brings the player up to a skill level where he can do it effortlessly in the game, where a crowd is heckling the player to miss. In any field, practice can be used to help one become better in the actual doing of that particular thing. For example, a speaker who practices speaking more than he actually goes out and stands in front of an audience to speak will become so comfortable from the drilling that when he actually goes out to speak he does so with no sweat.

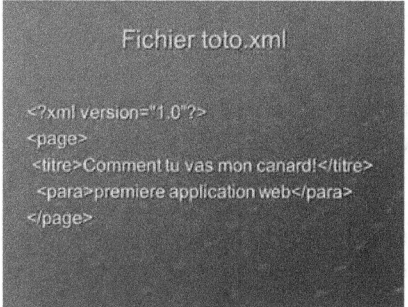

```
Fichier toto.xml

<?xml version="1.0"?>
<page>
  <titre>Comment tu vas mon canard!</titre>
  <para>premiere application web</para>
</page>
```

Chapter Ten: 10. Writing Code

To write code means to see the patterns and things and once you are able to do that, you can start writing your on patterns in the things you create, or you can take a pattern being used in one area and apply it to an entirely different field. An example would be the roadways of a city. From above, our road system is an imitation of rivers, running water. A strong case could also be made that the road systems are like veins in the body. This imitation has allowed civilization to advance. Where once the river was the root of transportation; now we find the Internet as the fastest route of transferring information, hence the name the information superhighway.

A pattern is simply a way something is. When you look at a pattern you have seen the way a thing functions and its form. A simple example of a pattern is a shirt. There are six basic parts to a dress shirt: 1. the collar, 2. The Placket, is the fabric that runs down the middle to cover the chest and back, 3. the cuff, 4. the sleeve, 5. the yoke, which covers the back neck and shoulders and 6. the tail, which falls below the waistline and is tucked into one's pants. This is the pattern we come to expect in this successfully made dress shirt. A suit follows the same pattern except material is heavier, thicker.

Examples of patterns would be a house. The house has the same things that every other house has, on a basic level. There is an exterior and interior of the house. On the exterior, you have walls, mostly four, in these walls are topped off by a roof. There are holes in the walls which are covered with glass, we call these windows. And there's normally a front door and sometimes a backdoor. That makes up the basic exterior of the house. The interior normally has a living room, a dining room, kitchen, one or more bedrooms, closets, and a bathroom. Those make up the basics of the interior of the house. If you were to walk inside of a house and there was no bathroom, you would not perceive it as being a completed house.

The same can be said of a car, thr exterior of the car as well as an interior of the car. The exterior has wheels, four. The exterior has doors with windows, a front with hood, bumper, headlights and window. The back has a trunk, and window. The interior has a front seat and a back seat. Carpeted floor, a steering wheel, gas and brake pedal. There is also a dashboard with a speedometer, fuel and temperature gages. There is a heating and air conditioning system and also a radio. That is the pattern of the car.

We also live our lives by patterns. We go to work at a certain time; we get off at a certain time. That could be called a time pattern, which is consistent with what has been done before. Without patterns, Man would actually be lost. Imagine walking into the grocery store for the very first time. The concept would be completely new to you. You would have a hard time navigating yourself around the store because there would be too many items pulling your attention. But because we are so used to the pattern of a grocery store, we understand how to proceed while inside. Every grocery store has its sections. We know when we want produce; we go to the produce section. We know when we are looking for dairy we go to the dairy section. When it's time to pay and leave, all stores have counters in the front of the store; those are the patterns of a store. Without these patterns in place each time one enters the store, he would have to reorient himself to his surroundings. But because we know the pattern we can walk in a given situation without having to rethink our next move. Some of the elements of a store would be such things as aisles that have signs above them. There are shopping carts to wheel around the merchandise one will purchase. There are shelves of products down the aisles. This is the standard of any store around the world.

Standard means a guideline or yardstick in which other things can be measured by. We know when something is out of place when it fails to follow the standard.

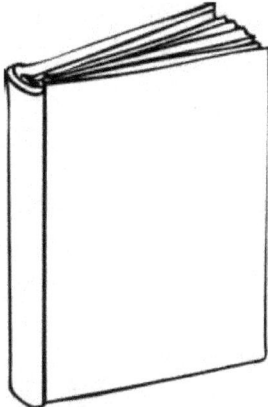

Closing

In closing, The Right Way is your roadmap to success. Its principles can be applied to any goal, large or small. It is a method by which one can achieve all of his hopes and desires and do so in such a systematic way that there is no room for doubt.

The Right Way is also your roadmap to happier relationships, more income and a better condition in life. Its tools will take you from where you are to places that you could only once dream of.

What The Right Way requires of you is simple: you must know where you want to go, more succinctly, what is the outcome you want to achieve. You must know its details; what it would sound like, smell like, and feel.

Next, you must look at where you currently are. Focus your attention on your surroundings. Don't dwell on it, but actually assess the situation. If your goal were to drive the golf ball 400 yards consistently, you would look at where your current drive range is. You would videotape your current swing; spot any overly noticeable outpoints in your stroke.

Thirdly, the Right Way requires that you build systematic steps to get yourself moving in the direction of your end goal. These steps are to be like a string of pearls, with one step naturally leading to the next.

In the end, The Right Way is the only way to get consistent results. Without it, you're just guessing and you will be met with more failures than successes.

So The Right Way is my gift to you. Use it. And never do it any other way, but The Right Way.

About the Author

John Conley is an entrepreneur and screenwriter. He has over fifteen years of business, management and organizational experience. He lives in Los Angeles, California.

www.ingramcontent.com/pod-product-compliance
Lightning Source LLC
Chambersburg PA
CBHW071828200526
45169CB00018B/1228